how2become

RAPID STUDY SKILLS FOR STUDENTS:
24 HOURS TO A FIRST-CLASS ESSAY
POCKETBOOK

**www.How2Become.com

Orders: Please contact How2Become Ltd, Suite 3, 40 Churchill Square Business Centre, Kings Hill, Kent ME19 4YU.

You can order through Amazon.co.uk under ISBN 9781912370450, via the website www.How2Become.com, Gardners or Bertrams.

ISBN: 9781912370450

First published in 2018 by How2Become Ltd.

Typeset for How2Become Ltd by Jacob Senior.

Disclaimer

Every effort has been made to ensure that the information contained within this guide is accurate at the time of publication. How2Become Ltd is not responsible for anyone failing any part of any selection process as a result of the information contained within this guide. How2Become Ltd and their authors cannot accept any responsibility for any errors or omissions within this guide, however caused. No responsibility for loss or damage occasioned by any person acting, or refraining from action, as a result of the material in this publication can be accepted by How2Become Ltd.

The information within this guide does not represent the views of any third party service or organisation.

CONTENTS

INTRODUCTION

Welcome to your guide, *24 Hours to a First-Class Essay.* In this book, you'll learn everything you need not only to complete your essay within 24 hours, but also to get the highest grade possible.

At university, it can be easy for deadlines to sneak up on you. Between studying, living your life, and any other responsibilities you might have as a student, you might just not have the time to devote to a long essay. Under optimal circumstances, we would recommend that you spend at least a week planning, researching, and writing your essay.

However, if you're reading this book, the likelihood is that one week doesn't exist.

In this book, we'll be taking a look at the *essential* aspects of a first-class essay, including the following:

- The process of writing an essay, from planning to submission;

- How to research an essay in a short space of time;

- An introduction to speed reading, packed with advice that you'll need in order to complete your essay within 24 hours;

- A guide to counter-arguments and criticism, an essential part of the essay-writing process;

- Expert tips on writing killer introductions and conclusions in the most efficient way possible;

- A guide to improving your memory so you can spend less time re-reading notes.

In this chapter, we'll take a look at what coursework at degree level is like, how to prepare for it, and how to complete it.

Bear in mind that, while most university courses have some kind of coursework during their duration, not all of them will. This means that, depending on your degree, university, and modules, you might not have to do any coursework. However, you might still find some of the information in this chapter useful when doing regular unassessed assignments on a weekly or fortnightly basis.

As previously mentioned, it's likely that you will have to complete coursework at some point during your time at university. In this chapter, we'll discuss how to navigate this form of assessment, so you can make your way to a first.

What is University Coursework Like?

If you've been through the UK's education system, it's almost certain that you've had to do coursework at some point. The best way to explain coursework in brief is to compare it to the other kind of assessment: exams.

Coursework differs from exams in a number of ways:

- Coursework assignments usually take place over a longer period of time. An exam is expected to be finished in a few hours, whilst coursework at university usually has a deadline falling weeks or even months in the future;

- Coursework at university often gives you more choice than an exam regarding the topic you'd like to work on. Exams might give you no choice of questions at all, whilst for coursework you might be given a few selected areas to write an assignment on;

- Depending on your subject, you will have to write your coursework to meet specified standards, such as referencing systems, and format. Most exams do not expect you to follow the same rules;

- A lot of exams are 'unseen', in that you don't know exactly what's going to appear in the paper until you begin the exam. For coursework, you usually have time to consider all of the possible topics, research them all, then choose the one you'd like to work on;

- Coursework is often continuous throughout the year, whilst exams tend to be situated at the end of a year.

Coursework at university is also different from school coursework in a few ways.

Firstly, school coursework tends to take a long time to complete: you might have had one or two pieces to complete in a single subject for the end of the academic year. In contrast, assignments at university are often handed in at the end of a term, and this means you'll have less time to complete each one. You need to keep this in mind when planning your time.

Additionally, university assignments are held to a much higher standard than those at school. You'll be expected to conduct independent research, using what you've learned in seminars and lectures as a springboard for your own ideas. You'll also usually be required to obey conventions that professional scholars would, such as referencing systems and suitable formatting.

Why Should I Bother?

At school, coursework might have only made up a small proportion of your overall mark. In a lot of cases, controlled assessments contribute to around 20% of one's grade in a subject. For some people, this isn't enough to warrant coursework receiving their full attention. Instead, they direct their efforts towards preparation for exams. We absolutely do not recommend adopting this same approach at university, for a number of reasons.

Firstly, assignments throughout the year often contribute to significant portions of modules. In essay-based subjects such as History, English Literature, or Theology, it isn't unusual for coursework to contribute up to half of a module's overall mark – even higher in some cases. This means that you *cannot* afford to slack when it comes to the assignments that you'll be given throughout the year. As mentioned in our chapter on planning your degree, information on how much each piece of coursework is worth should be made clear on department websites.

Another reason why coursework shouldn't be ignored is because it's a great way to secure marks for yourself throughout the year. Think of it this way: when you go into an exam, you don't really know exactly what's going to show up. This means that there's a margin for error – you might simply be unfortunate and get difficult questions. For coursework, this margin of error is often slimmer because you'll have more time to choose a topic, research it, get help from fellow students or staff if necessary, then write your response in your own time. This means that coursework assignments are a way of securing reliable marks, just in case the exam doesn't go so well.

Finally, the things you study for the coursework assignments might also appear in your final exams for the same module. This means that your assignments can be used as a form of practice or even revision. In some cases, it might even be worth looking back at your completed work while doing exam revision.

Types of Assignment

Depending on the course that you're studying, and the modules that you're taking, the type of assignment that you're given may differ. For example, Maths students might have to complete workbooks filled with exercises, whilst a History student will need to write essays on a given topic.

What most students will have in common is that they'll all have to complete a body of written work at some point, whether it's a lab report or a dissertation. Therefore, this chapter will focus on the written stages of coursework. However, some of these tips will apply to any kind of long-form work that you're completing.

Assignment Flowchart

The key to high grades in any assignment is planning. If you can nail a good plan and stick to it with all of your coursework, you can make sure that you cover all bases and increase your likelihood of excellence.

On the following spread is a flowchart designed to take you through the step-by-step process of completing an assignment – from the earliest stage of choosing a topic to submitting it and receiving feedback. You might find that some of the steps do not apply to the type of assessment that you're working on. In that case, skip the step and move onto the next one.

Let's take a quick look at each of these steps:

Choose a Topic

This will only apply to you if you've been given a choice of topic to write your assignment about. Essay-based subjects usually have a list of different questions that you can choose from, but this may differ between universities, departments, and modules. If you aren't sure, check the department website, or ask your lecturer or seminar leader.

Other subjects may be more limited in the range of topics you can write your assignment on. If this is the case, you can ignore this step.

Choose and Dissect Exact Question

Once you've chosen a topic, or been given one, you might be given a choice of the exact question. It might be tempting to jump to the question on the topic you most enjoy, but be cautious of the questions themselves. While they might cover the topic that you think you understand really well, they might approach it from an angle that you aren't comfortable with. Carefully examine each question available to you before choosing one.

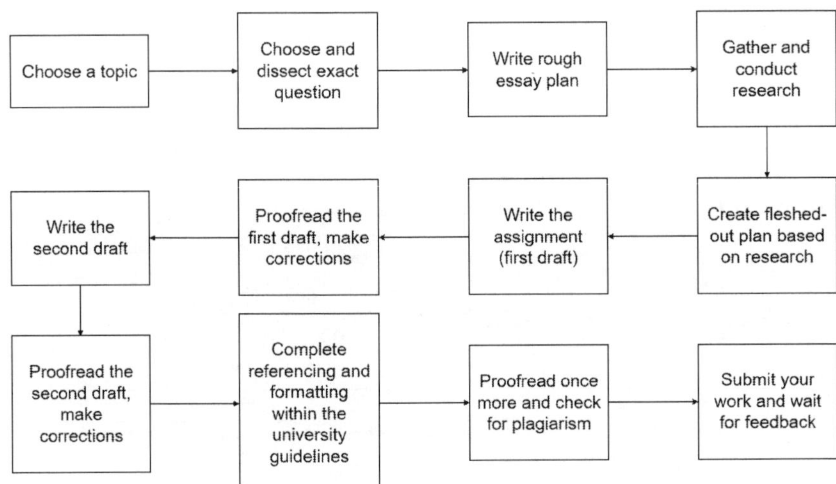

Choose a topic
Choose and dissect exact question
Write rough essay plan
Gather and conduct research
Write the second draft
Proofread the first draft, make corrections
Write the assignment (first draft)
Create fleshed-out plan based on research
Proofread the second draft, make corrections
Complete referencing and formatting within the university guidelines
Proofread once more and check for plagiarism
Submit your work and wait for feedback

After you've finished choosing a question, you need to take it apart and figure out what it's really asking of you. Keep an eye out for scope, both in terms of the scale of the area itself and how deep it expects you to go.

Write Rough Essay Plan

Once you've chosen your question and know what it's asking of you, it's time to start writing a rough plan. This won't be the final plan that you follow for the entire project – just a loose one to help you gather your thoughts for the research stage.

If you're writing an essay, try to construct a paragraph-by-paragraph plan in this stage. At the very least, you should have a good idea of what the sections of the essay or project are, and how they link together. Once you've finished doing this, you're ready to start the research phase of the essay-writing process!

Gather and Conduct Research

In this stage, you'll spend most of your time reading, working with others, or doing practical work so that you have something to support your assignment with. The exact nature of the research will depend on the subject and module that your assignment is in.

Create a Fleshed-Out Plan Based on Research

Once you've got all of your research together, you now need to apply it to your plan. If you're writing an essay, you want to look for anywhere in your plan where you've made some kind of claim. Add relevant evidence from your sources here so that everything you're going to write in your essay is supported.

If you're doing some other kind of assignment, such as a write-up based on lab work, your entire piece will centre around your research. Again, include evidence from your own research to your plan, where relevant, so your argument is well-supported.

To make things easier, try to make a note of all the page numbers and locations of everything you're citing in your work. This will save you from having to trawl through all your sources looking for the exact line and page where you got your evidence from.

Write the Assignment (First Draft)
Now that you've got a full and fleshed out plan, it's time to write the first draft. If you've taken your planning seriously, you shouldn't need to refer to any of your sources here – just follow each point of your plan, turning the bullet points and other short notes into full sentences.

If you've already made a full plan, this stage shouldn't take long at all. The key is to follow your plan as much as possible, and turn a series of notes into a coherent, eloquent piece of writing.

Proofread the First Draft

With a first draft finished, you should now read through it at least once. At this stage, keep an eye out for spelling, grammar, and punctuation errors – you don't want your work to contain any amateur mistakes.

Here, you can also get an idea of how your work flows from point to point. If you think some bits don't work properly, or something doesn't fit, make a note of it and then you can find a solution when you write the second draft.

Write the Second Draft

Writing the second draft is less a case of re-writing your whole assignment, but instead looking at the entire piece critically and trying to re-write parts so that they're even more concise. You might feel as though this is unnecessary, but going through and rewording things can help with clarity.

Proofread the Second Draft

As with the first draft, it's important to re-read your work to make sure there are no glaring errors.

Complete Referencing and Formatting

Hopefully, you've been referencing as you go along. If so, there should be little to do in this section. Just make sure that you've followed the referencing system that your university and department have specified, such as the Harvard Referencing System.

You will probably also need to write a bibliography – do this at this stage.

In addition, you should make sure that the formatting of your work meets the specifications of the department. If your work is word-processed, they might specifically request certain fonts, font sizes, and line spacing. Check the guidelines set by your department, since some universities will dock points from assignments that aren't formatted correctly.

Proofread and Check for Plagiarism

In this final stage, you want to proofread your work and specifically check for plagiarism. We'll discuss plagiarism in more detail later in this chapter, but for now ensure that whenever you've used supporting evidence from a source, you've cited them properly. The aim of this is to make sure that you aren't passing off someone else's work as your own.

One way to check for plagiarism is to copy and paste sections of your own writing into a search engine. If this leads to results of places where you might have gathered ideas from, then you need to cite it as a source or remove the suspicious piece of text from your work. If you do remove it, make sure to replace it with your own work.

Universities take plagiarism very seriously, so it's important that you take extra care when checking for it.

Submit Work and Wait for Feedback

Once you get to this stage, you're basically finished. However, you still need to submit your work. Different universities, departments, and even modules might specify how to hand in your work once it's finished. Some might request a printed copy, whilst others will use an automated system where you can upload your work to. In some cases, they might request both. Your department should make their requirements clear either on their website, or in the introductory documents for the course or module.

Once your work has been submitted, you'll need to wait for it to be marked. Hopefully this won't take too long, but different universities have different standards when it comes to turnaround on assessed work.

When your work and marks are returned to you, spend some time re-reading your assignment to see where you picked up marks, and where you lost them. Hopefully, the examiner has offered some feedback alongside the marked piece of work. Make sure that you read this feedback carefully and take it on board for your next assignment. If you don't get any feedback on your work, or would like more, get in touch with your seminar leader or lecturer.

How To Ace Your Coursework

Now that we've taken a look at the assignment flowchart and touched on each area, let's look at some expert tips for each major stage of the assignment-writing process.

Planning Your Coursework

In many ways, the planning stage of the assignment-writing process is the most important part of submitting an excellent piece of work. If you create a proper plan, then the bulk of the work you need to do will already be finished when you get to the main writing stage.

Treat the planning stage as though you were writing up the actual piece of work, but in a more condensed format. Try to create every point of your argument, with evidence and explanations, and put it inside your plan.

On top of this, divide these into paragraphs and sections, and make a note of ways in which each of them relates to the question and to the previous section. By doing this, you should create a plan that smoothly goes through every major point of your work. An essay or any other kind of written assignment which flows properly will have a much better chance of scoring high marks than one that feels clunky or disjointed.

As we've recommended in the flowchart above, you should try to create two plans for your coursework. The first is a rough plan that outlines the general direction of your argument, as well as some basic points. Once you've done all of your research, you can adapt this plan to create a more fleshed-out one.

Conducting Research

After planning, research is one of the most important parts of writing an assignment. No matter what course you're taking, if you fail to provide evidence for your argument then you will get very few marks. Without conducting thorough research, you won't have the evidence you need in order to create a piece of work that matches university standards.

A lot of the tips we suggested about how to work independently are relevant here. In particular, try to do the following when it comes to gathering information for your coursework:

Start by using recommended reading lists provided by the department. This will be a curated list of sources which are relevant to your topic. In addition, they *should* be books, journals, and other types of source which are suited to your level of study.

Make use of *reputable* online sources alongside books. By 'reputable', we mean journals and other works that have been formally published/peer reviewed.

Unless specified otherwise, try not to use amateur blog posts or online encyclopaedias. If you find a source that you aren't sure about, get in touch with your lecturer or seminar leader.

When it comes to research, you should have a wide range of resources available.

The first port of call should be your university library. Try to get hold of the most essential books from the recommended reading list as soon as possible, since these are the most likely to be taken out by someone else. Once you've got these, read the relevant chapters and take notes on anything that might be useful to your assignment, as well as the page numbers. Get all of the information you need as soon as possible, just in case the book gets recalled and you have to return it.

If you've exhausted all of the relevant materials in the library, get yourself online and see what you can access there. Quite often, universities will give you login details for online journals and journal search engines, giving you access to a wealth of articles and other material that might be useful for your work. Be sure to reference these correctly, since they must be cited in a slightly different way to print journals.

If you don't have access to any of these, some of the sources you need might be accessible in other places. In particular, extremely old works such as Ancient Greek philosophical texts can often be found in their entirety online and free of charge. Of course, more recent works will not be available in this way for copyright reasons.

If this doesn't cover everything, try and find some students on your course in the years above you. If you're lucky, they might have a copy of the book that you need that they could lend to you. If your university has a mentoring network set up between students across years, then this might be a great opportunity to get hold of key materials.

If there are still resources that you need after taking these steps, then you might have to buy the books yourself. When doing this, make sure you buy the correct edition of the book, since different publications of the same book might not be quite as relevant. This is especially the case for translated works, where there might be a large disparity between two separate translations. Reading lists set by departments and modules should include the exact versions you need if this is the case.

Once you have all of the sources you need, it's time to get reading and note-making. When it comes to coursework, it's often better to write out the key information in exact quotes. This is so that you don't exactly re-word something in a way which changes the meaning of the sentence. While you should almost always paraphrase rather than quote directly when writing your assignment, re-writing the quote in full at this stage is preferable. Remember to keep track of page numbers so that referencing is easier later on.

Although most research that students conduct involves reading and taking notes from articles, some courses might require lab work for assignments. In these cases, the work you will need to complete will be set out for you, and you'll likely be given a slot of time to do the lab work. Once you've finished it, you'll probably need to write a report on it. The tips in this chapter will apply to writing a lab report, but be sure to consult documents from your department which might specify conventions and formatting styles.

Once you've gathered all of the research you need, we strongly suggest adding the relevant information to your plan, fleshing it out even more. You might find that the plan you wrote before doesn't quite work in light of what you've learned from research. This isn't a problem: re-write your plan until it suits the kind of argument you want to make.

Writing Your Assignment

Once you've finished planning and researching, it's time to write your piece of work. If you've planned well, this shouldn't be too difficult a task; all you're really doing is turning short bullet points into full sentences. However, there are some tips you can take on board to improve your chances of getting the top grades.

Write the Introduction and Conclusion Last

Sometimes, figuring out a great introduction can be difficult. You want to avoid opening with grandiose, sweeping statements, but you also want to give a general idea of what your argument is. If you've planned properly, you should already know the shape and direction of your argument. However, it's usually better to jump straight into the main body of work. Then, you can write a fully focused and sharp introduction.

Once you've finished writing everything, then you can head back and write a great introduction and conclusion based on what's in the main part of your assignment.

Students often get stumped on their introductions, and aren't even sure where to begin. When you're on a tight schedule, you can't afford to sit looking at a blank screen waiting for ideas to come to your head. Start writing straight away and use this momentum to help you push through as much work as possible. Worry about the introduction later.

Keep Things Simple
You might be aware of the famous adage from *Hamlet* which states that 'brevity is the soul of wit'. In other words, you should not waste the reader's time; explain points properly, but in as few words as necessary.

In addition, you don't always need to use overly complicated terminology. In some cases, you'll have no choice, but in many cases simpler language is preferable. In some subjects, you might be marked specifically on the wealth of your vocabulary and your grasp on language. In these cases, you can be more decadent with your terms.

Another way to keep things simple is to use shorter sentences. The longer a sentence is, the more unwieldy it can become. In turn, this might lead to run-on sentences which are more difficult to read than shorter sentences. Experiment with the length of your sentences to see if making them shorter gives your work more clarity.

Adopt a Good Paragraph Structure

This tip is particularly important for students writing essays. Sometimes, it can be hard to keep a paragraph contained. Students can get carried away with their argument, until suddenly the paragraph contains a lot of complex points.

As a rule, you should try and keep paragraphs limited to one main point. This way, you can stop paragraphs from growing out of control, allowing the reader to understand your argument more easily.

A great way to make your paragraphs easier to follow is to treat each of them as a miniature essay. By this, we mean that each paragraph should have a short sentence which introduces the main point, followed by the point itself. Finally, you should end the paragraph with a short sentence which briefly summarises your point, and demonstrates how it relates to the question that you're answering. This way, you'll have your argument for each paragraph clearly laid out for the reader to see.

If it helps, you can try coming up with a subtitle for each paragraph in your essay. Don't include this in the finished copy, but writing each paragraph with the main point of it explicitly in mind will help you focus your efforts, and create a more consistent piece of work.

Once you have a paragraph structure like this, the flow of your essay will become a lot more pronounced. This means that you'll be able to spot parts that feel disjointed and correct their course. By 'disjointed', we mean parts of the essay which either stick out from the flow of your essay and don't lead to any new points, or sections which actively move against the flow of your essay.

Imagine your essay is a river. Each part of the essay should flow into the next part, as your argument cumulatively builds up towards the conclusion. The points made in earlier paragraphs should always contribute to later ones, and those which don't could be considered as irrelevant.

If paragraphs A, B, C, and D all support a larger argument made in paragraph F, but the argument in paragraph E has no bearing on it, then you need to consider whether it's paying off for you. If it isn't benefitting your argument, then you should probably get rid of it and use the space to write something relevant.

There's no set length that a paragraph needs to be, but they can be too long. If you have a single paragraph that's significantly larger than the rest in your essay, it might be worth revisiting it and seeing how you can divide it into smaller parts. This will prevent your essay from becoming 'bogged down'. Likewise, lots of tiny paragraphs can look too fragmented or poorly developed.

Referencing

Referencing is an essential part of most assessed projects. In particular, students studying for essay-based subjects should train themselves to reference sources properly so that their work looks professional and so they avoid accusations of plagiarism, which will be covered later in this chapter.

Depending on the university, course, and module, the type of referencing system that you'll have to use will differ. Some departments might be more relaxed about which referencing system you use, so long as you make sure that you are consistent. Your department should specify the referencing system that you need to use.

The following are some of the most prominent referencing systems in the academic world, as well as (roughly) which subjects they apply to:

Referencing System	Format	Example	Applicable Subjects	Notes
APA	Author (last name and initials). (Year of publication). *Title of book*. Place of publication: Publication.	Smith, J. (2013). *How to Reference*. London: How2become Ltd.	Social Sciences (e.g. Psychology or Sociology)	
Chicago	Last name, First name. *Title of book*. Place of publication: Publisher, Year of publication.	Smith, John. *How to Reference*. London: How2become Ltd, 2013.	History and Economics	
Harvard	Name of author(s) (last name and initials). (Year of publication). *Title of book*. Place of publication: Publisher.	Smith, J. (2013). *How to Reference*. London: How2become Ltd.	Arts and Humanities	Variant of the APA system.
MLA	Last name, First name. *Title of book*. Publisher, Year of Publication.	Smith, John. *How to Reference*. How2become Ltd, 2013.	Arts and Humanities	
Vancouver	Name of author(s) (last name and initials). *Title of book*. Place of publication: Publisher; Year of publication.	Smith, J. *How to Reference*. London: How2become Ltd; 2013.	Medicine and Science	

Bear in mind that the examples above only demonstrate how to reference a book with a single author. Each referencing system has different formats for each type of work that you're referencing. Here are a few examples:

Edited books	Books with multiple authors	E-Books and pdf documents	Specific chapters of edited books
Newspaper articles	Online newspaper articles	Journals	Online journals
Websites	Blogs	Online publications	YouTube videos
Films	CDs	Lyrics	Religious texts
Acts of Parliament	Press releases	Interviews	Patent documents
Social media	Apps	Podcasts	Maps
Unpublished works	Video games	Archived documents	Annual reports

Each referencing system will have its own rules regarding each of these types of source. Before including one of these sources in your work, find out the exact format.

It's also worth remembering that, when including citations in your work, you will need to cite sources as you go and include them in a bibliography.

The first of these is straightforward. Depending on the rules set by your referencing system or university, you will have to either cite sources *in-text* or by using *footnotes*.

Here's an example of an in-text citation in the Harvard referencing style:

Smith (2013, p. 135) notes that some universities prefer in-text citations.

This citation denotes the year that the book was published, as well as the exact page number it is referring to.

The alternative to the in-text method is to create a footnote. This is essentially the same as the in-text method, except the citation information appears at the bottom of the page:

In his book, Smith notes that other universities and referencing systems prefer the use of footnotes.[1]

The footnotes system is sometimes preferable because it can prevent the text from

---

1   Smith (2013), p. 136.

becoming too cluttered. Most word-processing programs are capable of automating the footnoting system, making it easy to do.

Once you've cited all of your sources in text and written your assignment, you'll need to construct a bibliography. This is a summary of all of the works that you've used when writing your own assignment.

Depending on your university and department, the contents of your bibliography will differ. Some prefer you to include everything that you've read regarding the topic of your assignment, even if you haven't referenced it in your work. Otherwise, they will ask you to only include works that you've referenced. Find out the conventions that your university has set before completing your bibliography.

Bibliographies should be filled out in alphabetical order by the surname of the author. So, 'Johnson, S.' would appear before 'Smith, J.'

A final tip for making referencing as easy as possible is to write a bibliography while you're gathering your research. This way, all you'll need to do is copy and paste the same bibliography into your assignment when you're finished with it. This is also a great method for keeping track of what you've read during the research stage, meaning you won't have to trawl back through your notes and books to find exact page numbers.

Proofreading

Proofreading is an essential part of the assignment-writing process for any kind of assessment. Whether you're solving Maths questions, writing an essay, or making a presentation, it's vital that you check for errors. You should look out for the following:

- Spelling, grammar, and punctuation errors;

- Inappropriate vocabulary;

- Unclear points;

- Messy paragraphs and sections;

- Sources without proper referencing;

- Factual errors.

Since this is a lot to keep an eye out for, you should probably do at least two proofreads of your work. On the first proofread, look out for the bigger issues, then move onto smaller errors such as typos in a later proofread, once you're happy with the content.

Another tip for proofreading is to wait for a little while after finishing a draft before reading it. If you start proofreading as soon as you've finished writing, you might be too burnt out to catch the issues. So, once you've finished writing your assignment, leave it for a couple of hours before taking a look at it. This way, you'll be looking at it with a 'fresh' pair of eyes, and you'll be more likely to spot things that need fixing.

Finally, if it's possible, have someone you trust take a look over your work. Even if they aren't an expert in the area you're writing on, they'll be able to tell you if there are spelling, grammar, and punctuation errors. Likewise, they'll probably be able to spot things which are unclear or messy. However, remember to be careful who you show your work to – someone might try to steal your ideas!

Plagiarism

Plagiarism is the act of taking someone else's work and, whether knowingly or unknowingly, try to pass it off as your own. This is an issue that universities take *extremely* seriously, and with good reason. Punishments for plagiarism will vary depend on the severity of the case, but it isn't impossible for them to end in expulsion from the university. For this reason, it's vital that you avoid plagiarism in your work.

As previously mentioned, one of the best ways to avoid plagiarism is to make sure that you correctly cite any information as a source. Think of it this way: if you got the idea from somewhere else, then you need to make that clear in your work. This is why you should make note of everything that you're reading for your assignment – you'll have a record of everything you've learned, and where you got it from.

Of course, it's very unlikely that any idea that you've come up with is completely original. The chances are that, at some point, someone else has thought of the same thing, and they might have even published it. In these cases, you should make use of search engines to look up what you've written, and see if there are reputable sources which support it. If this is the case, then you should cite this source in your work as evidence.

Ultimately, an assignment is about *your* ideas, not everyone else's. While it's important to include evidence for your ideas as much as possible, you must let your own ideas shine through. This might even be through analysing arguments made by other people. However, it's good to err on the side of caution when it comes to avoiding plagiarism.

Some universities have a plagiarism checker built into their submission systems. In particular, universities that use the online submission that we discussed earlier may have a plagiarism checker which automatically compares phrases and sentences in your work to content on the internet. If it finds a match, then you might be penalised for plagiarism.

In some cases, the plagiarism checker might be available to you as well. This can be a good way to spot if there's anything you've cited but forgot to reference properly. However, you shouldn't rely on this – your work should be fully referenced before you submit it.

Self-Plagiarism

Self-plagiarism is quite self-explanatory: it's when you've written something that you've already written in a previous piece of work. While it isn't treated as seriously as the usual type of plagiarism, it's still something that you can lose marks for.

For example, let's say that you wrote a Philosophy essay on utilitarian ethics. If you made the argument that utilitarianism is a poor ethical system because it can't guarantee what the outcome of an action will be, then this would be acceptable. However, if you wrote a very similar point in a piece of work you wrote later in the year – using the same examples, sources, and wording – you'd be at risk of self-plagiarism.

Some universities which use an online submission system will have a plagiarism tracker ready to use. If you've submitted work which is too similar, it could be flagged on the current piece of work that you're submitting. This usually isn't too much of a problem, since you're not likely to be making the same points across pieces of work. However, make sure that you absolutely do not copy from your previous work. In many cases, it probably won't even be relevant.

Submitting Your Work

Once you've finished your work and are happy with it, it's time to submit it. Depending on the university and subject, you might have to submit your work in different ways. Some universities use online systems, in which you'll need to upload a word-processed document containing your work. Usually, these systems allow for a plagiarism checker either on your own end or on that of the marker.

The other main submission system is the classic physical copy. In some cases, you'll need to supply your department with two copies of your work: one to be marked by the examiner, and the other to be archived for later reference. More and more universities are moving to digital systems because they're often easier to handle and help save paper, but be ready to submit a physical copy of your work if that's what your department requires.

Making Use of Feedback

Once you've got your work back, you'll hopefully have some feedback from the person marking it. One of the biggest mistakes students make when receiving their marked assignment is to check the score and then ignore everything else. Reading the feedback and making sure you incorporate it into your next piece of work is important whether you did well or poorly on the assignment.

If you got a great mark on the assignment, it's important that you know exactly what you did well. Sometimes, the thing that netted you marks might not be what you expected, so it's important to be clear. While you might have performed brilliantly, a good examiner will still try to suggest places where you could improve. Make sure you focus on these areas for your next assignment.

If you didn't do as well as you'd hoped to, you'll likely receive quite a few suggestions as to how you could improve. Take note of these because you'll almost certainly need to act upon them if you want to achieve a better grade next time. Remember that there should still be some areas where you've been given praise. Keep an eye out for these, because they'll provide some encouragement that you're getting some things right, and can certainly get better.

Remember that no assignment is perfect, and your examiners don't expect perfection. This is why you should keep an eye on what they suggest improving, as this will increase your chances of getting a higher mark in your next piece of work.

10 Tips for Getting a First in Your Essays

1. Read the question carefully and make sure that you understand it.

There's only one thing worse than realising you've misunderstood a question halfway through writing you essay, and that's realising you've misunderstood it *after* you get your marks back. Some people like to jump into an essay as soon as they've found a question that they think is interesting. However, by being too eager, students can end up either making more work for themselves when they have to re-write their entire essay, or lose marks because they didn't fully understand the question.

Having a strong understanding of your essay title will help you write the best answer possible. Pay attention to the scope of the question, and look at things such as timeframes. Additionally, make sure that you understand exactly what the question is asking of you. It's never a good idea just to throw everything you know at an essay. Think about what's relevant to the question being asked, then cater your knowledge to it.

2. Take planning seriously.

The best essays come about from meticulous research and planning. Some people spend only a little amount of time on the planning stage of their essay, leaving the bulk of the work for the writing stage. While this may work for some people, what you'll likely find is that you've forgotten something when planning and now have to find a place for it in your essay. This can result in a messy structure, and your essay can lose focus.

The best way to avoid this is to devote more time to the planning stage of your essay. Your plan should be as robust as possible, briefly detailing each section and paragraph. This way, you'll probably end up doing most of the work in the planning stage of the essay-writing process.

Once your plan is finished, and you're happy with the flow of it, then you should start writing the essay. You might find that the actual essay-writing part is easy – all you're doing is turning all of the points you've made in your plan into full-sentences and paragraphs. This also means that you can spot any problems with your essay in the earliest stage, before you've done the bulk of the actual writing. Finally, a strong essay plan will let you know where your argument is going before you've started writing, meaning you can tighten up your ideas rather than just make things up as you go along.

3. Make your essay laser-focused.

Don't *literally* write an essay on lasers. Instead, make sure that your essay is incredibly focused, since this will stop your work from trying to take on too much. Make sure you answer the question, but don't be afraid to take a narrow focus. It's almost always better to go in-depth on a small number of issues, rather than have a shallow analysis of lots of issues. At degree level, your work needs to have depth, so be willing to sacrifice breadth in order to get it.

For example, if a question requires you to use case studies to support your argument, consider looking at just one in more detail, rather than many in brief. This will also help you from going off on a tangent if you force yourself to narrow your focus.

Finally, having a very narrow focus gives you the opportunity to be original in a way that doesn't make sweeping generalisations. A very specific scope gives you the opportunity to go into detail on a minute area, which in turn might give you the chance to say something truly unique.

4. Be concise.

Flowery language and long words aren't always the most appropriate when writing an essay. Of course, you should have some kind of writing style, but this doesn't mean that you need to become incomprehensible. You should aim to make your language easy to understand, with sentence structure that doesn't spiral out of control. As a general rule, short sentences are preferable to longer ones, since you can prevent run-on sentences and a general lack of focus. The goal of an essay is to convey an argument, not to show off with fancy sentence structure. Be sensible and cut through nonsense.

5. Avoid clichés.

One of the most important things to remember when trying to get a first in your next essay is to avoid clichés. This is vital because whoever is marking your work doesn't want to be bored by the same ideas, phrases, and rhetorical devices. For instance, grand-standing is a cliché which detracts from the focus of an essay, and makes it more generic.

Here's an example of grand-standing:

*"Since the **dawn of human civilisation**, scholars have discussed what it means to be human…"*

While this might be the case, it's very unlikely that opening your essay with this phrase will be of any use to your argument. It doesn't shine any light on what you're going to say – all it does is wastes space which could be spent on meaningful discussion. Clichés like this don't come across as confident – it looks clumsy. As we mentioned previously, try and keep your argument to the point, rather than relying on rhetorical devices.

6. Paraphrasing is usually better than writing quotations.

At school, you might have been taught to quote from sources very frequently. While it's vital that you back up any claim that you make with evidence, a quote often isn't the best way to do so. Let's take a look at why.

When you use a quote as evidence, you'll probably be using it in the following format:

1. Introduce the point you want to make.

2. Give a quote to support the point.

3.   Explain what the quote is saying.

4.   Explain how this is relevant to your point, as well as the essay question.

When you explain what the quote is saying, you'll probably end up repeating some of the things that have been said. Therefore, you've wasted some space by writing the quote, then putting it in your own words. Instead, you can save space (and look more sophisticated) by ditching quotes and just paraphrasing instead. Not only does this save space, but it also proves that you understand the quote and know what you're talking about.

In some cases, however, it might still be relevant to include the full quote. For example, if you're quoting a line from a Shakespeare play, then the structure of the line, as well as the exact wording, is relevant. So, in these cases, you should opt to provide a quote in its entirety.

---

7. Make sure your referencing is correct and presentable.

When writing an academic essay, good referencing discipline is vital. Find out what system your university prefers (e.g. Harvard referencing, APA, MLA, Chicago/Turabian) and then stick to it strictly. There are plenty of referencing guides online which will show you to reference every kind of media possible – from written journals to YouTube videos. Go through your entire essay, and make sure that you've cited all of the sources you've used properly. This is an easy way to stop yourself from dropping some marks.

8. Be original.

Originality is a tricky area when it comes to writing an essay. The likelihood is that you're not going to be able to change the world in a single essay. Scholars devote their whole lives and thousands of pages to even the smallest of advances in their own fields. You've probably only got a few weeks and maybe a few thousand words.

Likewise, it probably seems as if all the big ideas have already been made. If you find yourself coming up with a radically new idea when writing an essay, the chances are that someone has already written about it. Being original can be incredibly difficult.

However, if you make your focus in an essay extremely narrow (as previously mentioned), you have a bit more room to work in. In a few thousand words, you aren't going to come up with a whole new theory. However, you might be able to make a small but meaningful difference within a narrow field. Trying to narrow your focus in your next essay in order to show some original thought.

9. Be confident.

Like originality, it's important to show confidence in your essays. After all, an essay is an argument, and the marker wants to see you get behind your ideas, rather than sit on the fence. You don't need to come across as foolhardy or blind to criticism, but don't be afraid to make strong claims if you have evidence to support them.

If you have space and time, try to address possible criticisms of your own argument. You can either address criticisms as you go, or devote a section towards the end of your essay on all the possible issues one might have with your ideas. Awareness of criticisms (as well as the ability to refute them) will show a level of sophistication that will put you far ahead of the competition.

10. Avoid lengthy introductions and conclusions.

Getting started on an essay is possibly the hardest part. Figuring out what you're going to say in the opening sentence can be a stumbling block, and it might be tempting just to start writing mindlessly. However, try to avoid this – you'll most likely ramble on, rather than getting to the point of your argument. Try to save introductions and conclusions for the very end of the writing stage of your essay. Once you know what you've said in the main body of your argument, you'll know what to write in the introduction and conclusion. This will help you to keep these sections laser-focused.

RESEARCHING IN 24 HOURS

One of the most essential parts of a first-class essay is good research. A solid foundation of research is absolutely necessary when writing an essay, since you'll need to be able to support all of your claims with evidence. Moreover, a strong backbone of research will help guide your argument to conclusions which follow logically, and are the most supported.

Research will also point you in the direction of interesting areas of discussion for your essay. Other scholars and writers might tackle an area which relates to an essay, and you might disagree with their conclusion. When writing a laser-focused essay on a topic, one of the best ways to approach it is to take a single idea and really dig into it. Researching will help you to discover these avenues for discussion.

When you've only got 24 hours to write your essay, the luxury of lengthy research isn't available. You'll need to read, write, and research quickly, and therefore you'll need all of the advice that you can get in order to succeed. In this chapter, we'll be taking a look at the following areas:

1. What independent study is and how to conduct it effectively.

2. Where to find research in a short space of time.

3. How to make the most efficient use of your research.

4. Tips for turning your research into solid points for your essay.

Time is of the essence, so let's get started!

What is Independent Study?

Before continuing, let's briefly touch on what independent study is. Independent study at university level can be broken up into the following areas:

- Independent research, such as finding books from the library to read for an upcoming seminar;

- Independent homework, such as a Maths workbook filled with problems to solve;

- Independent studying for a piece of coursework, such as an essay or lab report;

- Independent revision for exams.

By independent study, we mean any study that isn't overseen by a teacher, lecturer, or seminar. For many students, independent study will occupy the majority of their time. Others, however, will have less independent work to do.

For example, students studying Maths will generally have a lot of contact hours (lectures and seminars). While they'll have a lot of independent work to do on top of this, they'll generally have less independent study than students taking Humanities degrees.

A student studying History, for example, will have far fewer contact hours. Because of this, these students will be expected to read much more on their own time. While this might not balance out perfectly between Science degrees and Humanities courses, the general rule is that the fewer contact hours you have, the more independent work you'll be expected to do.

Conducting Research Alone
Conducting independent research is useful for any subject, but vital for those studying degrees with fewer contact hours. This is because these students will have a lot more work to do on their own time.

If you're studying one of the Humanities or Social Sciences, then you'll have to do a lot of reading on your own, usually on a daily basis. This could be set reading for a seminar or lecture, or just general reading to get you ahead in your next piece of coursework. Whatever the case, you'll need to be able to work on your own in order to stay ahead of the game and improve your chances of getting a first.

When it comes to almost any module, you'll probably be given a list of sources which will be relevant to you. This tends to consist of the following:

1. **Core sources.** These are usually text books or primary reading, with the suggestion that you should purchase these for yourself since you'll be referring to them often.

2. **Further core texts.** Typically, these are available in the university library, or the lecturer will be printing handouts of specific chapters.

3. **Seminar sources.** These are usually set by your seminar leader, but can also be set by lecturers too. In a lot of cases, these will be made readily available via printed handouts or digital copies, unless they are already easily accessible online.

4. **Further reading.** These sources are usually reserved for students writing about a specific topic within the module. When it comes to completing assignments at the end of term, you'll want to find the further reading that's suitable for your module. If you aren't writing your coursework on this topic, you probably won't have to worry about this until the end of the year when it comes to exam revision.

Try to complete your reading in this order. Start with the 'core' works since they are usually picked for being the best introduction to a module or topic, with the reading becoming more specialised over time.

In addition to these areas, it might be worth looking at companion pieces to core texts. This is particularly useful for Humanities subjects such as English Literature, Philosophy, or History. If you're reading a core text written a long time ago, it might be helpful to read a secondary source which helps you contextualise it. For example, if you're reading *The Odyssey*, it would be handy to have a secondary work that you can read alongside the main text.

This way, you'll be given additional insight into the primary source, which will make understanding it much easier. This won't be relevant for all courses, and not all of your primary texts will have companion pieces. However, this will be incredibly useful for the modules that do.

Finding Your Research

The first thing you need in order to conduct your research is some material. Under ideal circumstances, you'd have pages upon pages at your disposal, but you probably don't have the time for that. So, we've made a 'map' of the route you should take through your research if you're strapped for time.

Note: In most essays, you'll need to reference all of the points you take from other sources, and any evidence from your research. You'll have to be diligent in your referencing to avoid accusations of plagiarism. We've already discussed referencing on pages 31 to 36. In order to save time, try to make note of your sources and the relevant page numbers as you go through your research. This will save you from a panicked rush at the end of the essay-writing process – something you simply don't have time for!

Lecture/Seminar Notes

The first stop should be any notes, slideshows, and other materials given to you in seminars and lectures. While these aren't definitive in any way, they'll give you a basic understanding of the topic you're writing about. If you attended the lecture/seminar and managed to take your own notes, you should take another look at these before you start planning your essay.

In addition to the content of the lecture and seminar notes, keep an eye out for any recommended reading or additional materials which were mentioned or included in lecture notes. These should be your next step after re-reading the lecture and seminar notes.

When it comes to reading these extra materials, remember that you don't have all of the time in the world to leisurely read through it all. If the piece is particularly long, try to skim or search through it for the most relevant and important information. If the material is on the computer, use the search function (CTRL + F for Windows PC, CMD + F for Mac) and enter keywords to help you find the important details. If the material is a book, find the index and make use of that. The last thing you can afford at this point is to sit and read through interesting, but ultimately irrelevant, information.

Online Journals and Articles

Once you've read and understand the basics of the topic, you're ready to move on to online journals and articles. Hopefully, your lecturers, seminar leaders, or tutors have given you a reading list for the topic that you're writing about. You should start by skim-reading these, looking for keywords and key points. Take note of these as you go.

Once you've quickly read the sources given to you by your lecturers, you need to branch out in order to write an impressive essay. The sources given to you aren't worthless – far from it – but if you want to create a unique and nuanced argument for your essay, you need to find something more obscure.

Think about it this way: whoever is marking your essay is probably also examining five, ten, or even fifty other essays on the same subject matter. While the examiner is looking for a strong argument and sophisticated writing, they're also on the lookout for something that is unique. Therefore, it pays to write an essay that discusses the topic from an unexpected, but ultimately insightful, angle. We'll discuss this in more detail in our section on "turning research into essay gold." For now, keep uniqueness in mind when reading your research.

Articles found online are great for creating a unique essay since you'll be introduced to a broad range of what we might call 'fringe' ideas. The books in your university library and those recommended to you by your lecturers will likely be more mainstream. These sources will cover overall topics and supply the framework for a strong argument, but at best will only point in the direction of where to find more nuanced and unique angles to view an essay question from.

This is where online resources really shine. Your university should have access to some kind of online resource database, such as JSTOR (www.jstor.org). These databases are packed with essays from journals, articles, and other sources on an immensely wide range of topics. What's best of all is that, provided that your university has bought access to it for students, you can use this service for free. This means that you don't even have to worry about buying books for your essays; you can make use of these articles that are now at your disposal.

One thing to be careful of when using online resources for research is that not all sources are born equal. Simply put, some sources will be considered more trustworthy and academically appropriate than others. Using an online database of journals and articles will almost guarantee that the sources you are using are appropriate for use in your essay, since almost all of the content has been written by professionals and academics for the purpose of inclusion in journals. Since many of these journals are held in high regard, the sources that you will be reading are excellent for basing your essay on.

If you're having trouble finding great articles on your essay topic in the database, you can go directly to a relevant academic journal's website and access the articles and essays there. In some cases, you'll be able to log into the online database that your university has subscribed to, meaning that you'll get free access to the journals.

If you can't get access to them for free, try and see if there are printed copies in the university library.

Books

Obviously, books are one of the key locations for conducting research when it comes to essay planning and writing. However, when you're writing an essay in 24 hours, you don't necessarily have time to read a whole book on a single topic.

However, this isn't to say that books are completely useless when you're writing an essay under time constraints. There are plenty of academic books which are broken up into a variety of viewpoints and discussions on a single topic, sometimes written by multiple different authors. These anthologies are invaluable for writing a strong essay, since they'll provide lots of different angles to view the essay topic from. While you don't need to (and shouldn't try to) discuss every single perspective on a topic, these will provide you with a lot of context, as well as potential criticisms and counterarguments that you can draw from.

Along with reading books, you can often find 'reviews' of academic books on the online databases which we've previously discussed. These aren't quite the same as a review of a film or a television series in that they are a buyer's guide. Instead, critical and academic reviews serve as a summary and brief critical analysis of the text. These are a great way to get an understanding of a text without having to read it in full. However, be careful when treating these reviews as gospel, as they are essentially an interpretation of the text. The best thing to do is to read it yourself.

Efficient Research

No matter your circumstances, it's always beneficial to be efficient in your research. However, you've only got 24 hours to research, plan, write, and proofread your essay. This means that you need to be saving as much time as possible. Let's take a look at some ways which can help you save time during the research stage of the essay-writing process.

Search Functionality

As previously mentioned, using the search functionality during research will save you a lot of time. For digital texts, CTRL + F (or CMD + F on Mac) will often be your go-to method of searching. Try to use keywords which can be found in your essay question, or in any lecture or seminar notes given to you by the department. Try to think laterally about these keywords, since some terminology might not be universal.

If you're using physical books, you'll have to make use of the index. Again, keywords are important here as they'll point you in the right direction as quickly as possible.

Read Synopses, Abstracts, and Reviews to Guide You

You won't have enough time to read through an entire book or lots of articles. So, the best thing to do is to find out exactly what it is you need to read. Whether it's specific chapters of a book or specific texts from a journal, you can use synopses to highlight what the resource will cover, and whether or not that matches your area of study.

In addition, you can use the abstract or introduction of a text to inform whether it will be useful or not. In particular, the abstract of a paper will outline the entire 'map' of the argument, giving you an idea of how useful it will be to you.

Use Companions to Help Your Understanding

Companions are books written by a secondary source with the intention of aiding the understanding of another book. For example, your essay might require that you read *The Odyssey*. While reading the primary text is important, it might be difficult to understand, and some details might be lost on you without the prerequisite context. This is where a companion text comes in useful. These books, written by experts on the source material, provide additional insight and interpretation that will be incredibly useful when writing an interesting and nuanced essay.

If the primary text has been translated from another language, particularly an ancient language, the translation might be incredibly dense and difficult to follow. Companion texts are great for re-writing the key points from the source material and making them more digestible.

If you're short on time, you shouldn't try to read the entirety of the primary text as well as all of the companion book. Instead, try to focus on key sections of both which are explicitly relevant to your area of study.

Alternatively, you can use a combination of the companion text and a synopsis of the primary source to give yourself a good idea about what the primary text is about.

Share Notes with Friends

If you have any friends or course-mates who are writing about the same or a similar topic, try and get in contact with them and see if they're willing to share notes with you. At the very least, try to have a discussion with them about the topic, since their ideas will probably give you some avenues for discussion in your own essay. However, remember not to share too much, as this could appear in your essay as plagiarism of some kind. Ultimately, the examiner wants to see **your** ideas, not someone else's.

Turning Research into Essay Gold

Once you've collected all of your research notes, you need to turn it into a killer essay. Here are a few ways in which you can do this.

Find a 'Back-and-Forth' Narrative and Join in

Sometimes, you might find that the essay topic you're writing about is dominated by two or three major theories, ideologies, or perspectives. You might find that, in your research, there's a 'back-and-forth' between these sides, resulting in a conversation that you can follow from essay to essay, book to book, and so on. In some cases, journals deliberately follow up one essay with another which directly opposes it, creating a discourse that you can easily get involved in.

As we've previously discussed, you can't exactly take both sides in an essay. Rather, you need to pick a side and defend it or attack it. The best way to do this is to read through the most relevant parts of this 'back-and-forth' and find an area that you can latch on to and either attack or defend. This brings us to our next point.

Use Your Research to Focus Your Essay

As mentioned in a previous chapter, having a laser-focused essay is the key to getting a first both in an individual piece of coursework and overall in your degree. The examiner would much rather see you focus heavily on a narrow area of discussion than present a shallow analysis of a broad range of topics. In other words, depth is more important than breadth in most essays.

With this in mind, it's important to think of ways in which you can use your research to make your essay focused on a very specific area. The best way to do this is to read through a text, and choose a single argument for or against an idea that is directly relevant to your essay title, and then focus your entire essay on that. It requires discipline, but if you can write a two-thousand word or three-thousand word essay on this single area, your essay is going to have a lot more depth than one which broadly strokes over the entire topic.

Use Your Research as a Road Map

As previously mentioned, one of the ways you can effectively use your research is to use it as a guide. Your research should demonstrate a clear debate between two or more competing ideas or theories; now it's your job to take what's relevant from them to create a complete argument. Here's an example of how you might want to use your research to support your argument:

Introduction: Use your research to give brief context for the question that you will be answering.

Argument 1 (or part 1 of your overall argument): Start with the initial basis of your argument, then use supporting evidence to reinforce this starting point. Then, provide a counterargument or criticism, giving it supporting evidence or a citation. Finally, refute this counterargument or criticism with more supporting evidence for your own argument.

Argument 2 (or part 2 of your overall argument): With the foundation of your argument in place, look at what logically follows from your initial premise. Alternatively, look what the outcome of your refutation of the counterargument is. Provide further evidence for the new claim that you're making. Again, you can provide a counterargument and refute it here to strengthen your essay.

From here, you can continue this approach for argument points three, four, five, and so on. The trick is to constantly support any claim that you make with evidence. This way, your argument is always backed up by evidence. Your research becomes the backbone of your entire argument, giving it weight and credibility throughout.

SPEED-READING

In this chapter, we are going to run through several techniques that speed readers use to save time on every sentence, paragraph, and page they read. Throughout, you will also have the opportunity to practise your new skills on sample writing extracts. Let's begin with a basic first step, which represents the foundation of many other speed reading techniques: reducing sub-vocalisation.

Reducing Sub-Vocalisation

The first step you should take when aiming to increase your reading speed is to reduce sub-vocalisation. Let's start by discussing what this means! While 'sub-vocalisation' sounds complicated, it's actually quite a simple concept to grasp. You'll already be familiar with it – it's what most people do whenever they read anything!

In short, sub-vocalisation is the act of sounding out the words in your head, or 'silently speaking' as you read, in accordance with the way most of us were taught to read at primary school. While this is logical and helps children with comprehension, it is possible to suppress this instinct in order to increase your reading speeds.

There are a few methods you can use to reduce sub-vocalisation. The most straightforward way to do so is to practise using rapid and jerky eye movements ('saccades') to get through a sentence, rather than one smooth 'tracking' motion that you might currently be doing. This means that you are only actually looking at a few words in a line, and letting your peripheral vision catch the rest.

Not looking at every word like this will mean that you are sub-vocalising far fewer words – only the ones you are focusing on – but are still reading and understanding everything. Saccadic eye movements ensure that your brain does not have the time to sound out each word; you'll have moved onto the next line before it has the chance. Of course, this reduces the amount of time it takes to finish what you're reading!

Another means of reducing sub-vocalisation is to 'distract' yourself while reading, by thinking about other things at the same time you are reading the text in front of you. One way to do this is by listening to ambient music that doesn't have lyrics. It is difficult to do, but with practice you will eventually be able to train your brain to 'listen' to the music rather than the 'sounds' of sub-vocalisation, and increase your reading speed this way.

Similarly, one technique involves counting in your head while reading. Sub-vocalising numbers rather than the words you wish to read may help you, as you will be forced to read without sounding the words out in your head. However, this may not work for everyone – make sure you are still taking in what you read. Experiment with this to see if it gets you results – perhaps you'd be best advised using this technique with text you only have to skim-read.

Rapid Serial Visual Presentation (RSVP)

Now, this technique is especially useful for smartphone, tablet, laptop, or computer reading. Essentially, it involves the use of downloadable programmes that are able to transmit your reading material to you one word at a time. This is how it works: the words flash up only once before the programme moves on to the next one. Within many of these programmes, which you can get by downloading applications online, you can set the speed at which the words appear and disappear. For example, you can set it so you are reading 10 words per second. This flexibility allows you to set reading targets within time limits. So, say you need to read a 6,000-word document, and want to get through it in 10 minutes. You know you'll be able to do this if you set your application to show you 10 words per second.

The point of such programmes is to eliminate regression (looking backwards) and force you to maintain high reading speeds. While RSPV is still considered to be an experimental method of speed reading, it is certainly a method to try out to see if it works for you. Perhaps start using it with something you only need to skim-read, and see if you can still remember/understand what you've read after it's over. One disadvantage is that it may be long-winded to stop the programme mid-way through a piece of writing to navigate backwards and look at a particularly important or interesting passage. So, if you need to collect direct quotes for an essay, perhaps stick to more conventional methods!

Meta Guiding

'Meta guiding' is a very simple and proven speed reading strategy, and one you may be familiar with already. Essentially, it involves using your finger to trace underneath the words you are reading. The point is to move your finger at a faster speed than you would normally read, forcing your eyes to follow and read faster than normal! Of course, you do not necessarily have to use your finger; you could use a pen, stylus, or any other implement you see fit.

Meta guiding is effective for one main reason: it reduces the chances of regression, i.e. looking back over what you've already read. Regression is bad a few reasons – it means you are not reading well enough to understand what you're looking at the first time around, and it slows you down. Meta guiding will ensure that you are reading every line, and that you are constantly progressing through what you're reading.

Meta guiding is also good because it is easy to start practising. Start with a slowish speed, only slightly faster than you naturally read, then work your way out of your comfort zone. With a bit of practice, you will surprise yourself with how well you can keep up with your finger, even if it is going improbably fast. If you find yourself tempted to look ahead of your finger, or onto the lines below, you can use a sheet of paper to block out what's underneath the line of text you are reading. This will ensure that you are focusing on the correct line, and that maximum comprehension is maintained.

Scanning

Let's say that you are writing an essay with the title: "Leon Trotsky was the most important factor in the Red Army's victory over the White Army in the Russian Civil War. Discuss." The first step would be to unpack what this prompt is asking of you. In doing so, we can determine the following things:

1. You need to explore Trotsky's contribution to the Civil War victory i.e. points that 'agree' with the statement given.

2. You need to explore the other factors that contributed to the Red Army's victory/ the White Army's loss.

3. You need to personally take a side in this debate – if you don't think it's Trotsky, what factor was most important?

So, when reading for this topic, say in a textbook about the Russian Civil War, you should go about it in the following way. Speed read your resources, but with a few 'key words' in mind. For example, 'Trotsky'.

COUNTER-ARGUMENTS AND CRITICISM

When researching, planning, and writing your argument, you're going to come up against criticisms, counterarguments, and objections to the position you're trying to defend. If you want to be taken seriously at an academic level, you need to be prepared to address these responses to your argument.

Responding to counterarguments is, in itself, an art form. In this chapter, we'll take a look at how to deal with counterarguments and criticism by examining the following areas:

1. When to discuss counterarguments in your argument.

2. How to present counterarguments in your own work.

3. How to refute counterarguments in your own work.

When Should I Discuss Counterarguments?

Once you reach the planning stage of your argument, you have a choice of how to approach counterarguments. Some people choose to respond to counterarguments immediately where they are relevant. Take a look at the following structure:

Introduction

Argument 1

Counterargument to Argument 1

Response to Counterargument (for Argument 1)

Argument 2

Counterargument to Argument 2

Response to Counterargument (for Argument 2)

The benefit of this approach is that you can raise counterarguments as you go, and so the content in question will still be fresh in the reader's mind. You can do this throughout your argument, allowing your responses to the counterarguments to build cumulatively to your central thesis.

Alternatively, you can save all of the counterarguments until the end of your essay. Here's the structure for it:

Introduction

Argument 1

Argument 2

Argument 3

Argument 4

Counterargument to Argument 1

Response to Counterargument (for Argument 1)

Counterargument to Argument 2

Response to Counterargument (for Argument 2)

Counterargument to Argument 3

Response to Counterargument (for Argument 3)

Counterargument to Argument 4

Response to Counterargument (for Argument 4)

Conclusion

Sometimes, approaching each counterargument as you go can get overly convoluted. The above structure allows you to make things more clear-cut, as long as you specify which argument the counterargument is addressing.

Depending on what you're studying, one approach might be preferable to another. If you aren't sure which is more relevant, ask a relevant member of school or university staff which would be more acceptable.

How to Present a Counterargument

Once you've decided on where you're going to address counterarguments, you need to consider how to frame them properly. If your writing isn't clear, some readers might get confused about whether you support or wish to refute a counterargument that you're presenting. To avoid this, you should introduce a counterargument in the same way that you would approach one of your own points:

1. Provide a short introductory sentence which presents the counterargument.

2. Explain what the counterargument is.

3. Demonstrate how it is relevant to, or how it may damage, the argument you're presenting.

This level of signposting will clearly highlight that this is a counterargument that you want to address, which we will cover in the next section. First, let's consider some other ways in which you can make your presentation of counterarguments even more sophisticated.

Mention the Person (or People) Who Coined It

In an academic argument, the counterarguments you raise should be attributed to a relevant scholar. By attaching their name to their work, you're doing three things:

1. Avoiding plagiarism by not trying to pass off other people's ideas as your own.

2. Demonstrating that you are aware of the wider debate and that you've read work from other writers, not just the primary individuals in question.

3. Giving your reader or audience a place to look for more information if they find your own argument interesting.

So, referring to the individual responsible for the counterargument that you're addressing is incredibly worthwhile. Make sure to cite them properly, using whichever referencing system your school or university specifies.

Present the Counterargument Honestly

When presenting a potentially troublesome counterargument, you may be tempted to present it in a format which is easy for you to tackle. While this might seem like a smart idea, the reality is that you're playing into a trap that any marker or astute opponent will spot immediately. In these cases, you'd be 'putting up a straw man'.

> To 'put up a straw man' is to misrepresent your opponent's argument, whether intentionally or not. This can involve oversimplification in order to make the opponent's argument easier to attack, or make the argument look more extreme than it actually is.

Essentially, if you misrepresent someone else's argument, you can't combat it effectively. So, when it comes to criticising your overall argument, you'll be accused of 'dodging' the real problems being highlighted by counterarguments. For this reason, take extra steps to present counterarguments as accurately as possible.

How to Refute a Counterargument

Now that you know where and how to present a counterargument, you need to be able to refute it. After all, there's no point including a criticism of your argument to your essay if you have no way of defending yourself!

Refuting a counterargument can be incredibly difficult, especially if you're new to the subject that you're writing about. When you're focusing on your own argument, it can be hard to find the time to research why a certain counterargument is ineffective. This is why we suggest taking potential counterarguments seriously when researching and planning your own argument.

Let's take a look at some tips for how to refute counterarguments in your own essay or verbal argument.

Pick Your Battles

When writing an argument, there are two things you need to bear in mind regarding counterarguments:

- You can't beat them all.

- Even if you could, you probably don't have time to.

For these reasons, you need to choose the counterarguments you want to address or refute. Ideally, this should be done in the planning stage of your essay or argument, so that you know which counterarguments and criticisms are relevant. Once you have an idea about what you're up against, you can then decide which counterarguments you would like to address.

Make sure you don't pick the most fatal counterarguments unless you have the evidence to support yourself, since you'll waste time planning for an argument that you can't win. Likewise, don't set up easy counterarguments to knock down – you won't impress anyone this way. Find counterarguments that you have the evidence to defeat, but that will also require effort to properly contest.

As a rule, you shouldn't refute a criticism that you haven't properly explained. If you want to contest a counterargument, spend at least one paragraph laying the groundwork for your response by introducing and explaining it sufficiently. Conversely, you should try to avoid introducing a counterargument without refuting it.

You should acknowledge potential counterarguments even if you aren't going to combat them, but give proper reason for it, such as a lack of space or time. This way, the reader won't be surprised by counterarguments appearing out of nowhere. Equally, this means that they won't be left disappointed, because they thought you were going to address a counterargument, only for you to never return to it.

Use Evidence

When it comes to refuting a counterargument, you need to have evidence on hand to prove it wrong. The type of evidence will depend on the area that you're studying. For example, if you're writing a scientific paper, then you'll need to draw upon peer-reviewed data to demonstrate how a counterargument is incorrect. If you're in the area of Philosophy, your evidence is going to be a lot more abstract – focusing on thought experiments, logical inconsistencies, and fallacies. Choose a form of evidence which is suitable for your area of study.

If you've planned effectively, you should already possess the evidence that you need in order to refute a counterargument. You don't need to completely bury the criticism in evidence – just present the strongest piece of data which puts the counterargument into question. Here's an idea of how you might structure your response to a counterargument using evidence:

1. Summary of why the counterargument is false.

2. Deeper explanation of why the counterargument is false, including evidence.

3. Explanation as to how this affects your initial argument (if at all).

4. Always keep in mind that, without evidence, responses to counterarguments are empty.

Conclusion

Now you should have a clear idea about how to deal with counterarguments in written essays in verbal arguments. When addressing counterarguments and criticism, try to keep the following in mind:

1. You can address counterarguments either immediately after raising your own argument, or wait until the end of your essay to address each criticism.

2. Present your counterarguments with a similar structure to a usual argument.

3. Present counterarguments as accurately as possible, and avoid putting up a straw man.

4. Don't try to take on every possible counterargument – choose the most relevant ones and focus on them.

5. Make use of evidence that fits your area of study, in order to contest a counterargument.

INTRODUCTIONS AND CONCLUSIONS

You may have noticed that we've waited until one of the final chapters to discuss two of the most important parts of any argument: the introduction and conclusion. This is because we believe that introductions and conclusions are best saved for the end when constructing your argument. In this chapter, we'll explain why this is the best course of action, as well as how to put together the best introductions and conclusions to make your arguments even stronger.

What's the Point of Introductions and Conclusions?

While the most important part of any argument is the substance in its main body, you need the right 'frame' for your masterwork to go in. Introductions and conclusions serve this function, as they provide the set-up and summary of your argument respectively.

Jumping straight into the main body of your work is a great way to get started with an argument, but that doesn't mean you should neglect introductions and conclusions. Without the correct framing by the introduction and conclusion, your argument might lack focus or context. Therefore, it's vital that you take the time to learn how to use them effectively.

As the name suggests, the purpose of an introduction is to 'introduce' your argument to the reader, audience, or your opponent. It needs to provide some context of the ensuing argument: why the argument is important, and other questions which might influence or be influenced by your own. If your argument is specifically a response to another made by someone else, then it might also be appropriate to give a summary of it in the introduction. We'll take a closer look at writing the perfect introduction later in this chapter.

As for conclusions, the overall aim is to bring your argument to a close. The conclusion is usually a summary of what you've already said or written, tying your argument in a nice bow so that it flows well. We'll discuss conclusions further later in this chapter; but one thing to bear in mind is that you should *never* introduce whole new ideas in your conclusion. If you think there's something relevant that you missed, go back and find space in the main body of your argument and add it in.

Why Should I Write Them Last?

It might seem a bit peculiar to form your introduction at the very end of your argument, but we have good justification for this. Since the introduction and conclusion of your arguments introduce and summarise the main body of your work, you need to have a precise idea about what your argument actually contains before you can give a satisfactory primer or recap of it. By all means, get a rough idea of what you'll say in your introduction and conclusion before writing them, but having a completed body of work finished first will make it much easier to refine them.

The other reason why it's a good idea to write your introduction and conclusion last is because it means you can jump straight into developing your ideas. Coming up with a killer introduction leaves a lot of writers stumped, so skip it for now and head straight for the main argument. Then, once you have your whole argument laid out, you can head back to the beginning and entice the reader with a great introduction.

Now that you know why it's a good idea to leave the introduction and conclusion until the end of the argument-writing process, let's look at how to tackle them.

Onto the Scene – Constructing a Stellar Introduction

When writing an introduction, we find that the following three aspects should be kept in mind:

1. **Clarity** – Your introduction needs to clearly set out the area of debate that you're covering. Briefly explain what makes your position so important, as well as what your argument actually is.

2. **Accuracy** – Make sure that your introduction is razor-sharp. By this, we mean that you should focus only on what's necessary for your argument. This way, the reader or audience has a strong idea of the direction that your argument will take. Try and lay out the main points of your argument in brief during your introduction.

3. **Brevity** – Don't waste the reader or audience's time, and don't waste your own

space. The introduction needs to be fairly brief – quickly outlining everything we've spoken about in the above two points.

As you can see, introductions are at their best when they're to-the-point and cut out nonsense. For this reason, we absolutely recommend that you avoid what is known as 'grand-standing' – setting up your argument in grandiose but ultimately pointless terms. Here's an example of grand-standing in the introduction of an argument or essay:

"For thousands of years, scientists, philosophers, and theologians alike have all pondered on the origins of humanity."

Simply put, this isn't a very sophisticated way to open your argument. This introductory sentence adds very little to what you're trying to say, and probably bears no relevance to the rest of your argument. Instead, try and cut straight to the chase. If you're writing an essay, you might want to open like this:

*"The aim of this argument is to demonstrate how advances in our understanding about human origins weren't **revolutionary**, but in fact **evolutionary.**"*

Here, the goal of this argument is neatly summed up by a sentence which gets to the point, is accurate in its terms, and doesn't grand-stand unnecessarily. It also has the added benefit of sparking the audience's imagination, setting them up for the rest of the introduction which will go into slightly more detail.

Once you've nailed your opening sentence, it's time to look a bit closer at what you're arguing about. If you're new to writing arguments, you might want to keep things simpler, rather than get flashy with fancy techniques. **Remember our three rules: clarity, accuracy, and brevity.** Then, apply them to the following steps.

Clearly show what it is you're arguing for, and what approach you're going to take. This should be a single, continuous line of argument. If you want, you can lay out each step of your argument here. This will give sufficient signposting to the reader or audience so that they can follow your argument more easily.

Briefly make note of possible criticisms of your argument, and either specify whether you will approach these as you go, or tackle all of them towards the end of your argument. When giving verbal arguments or presentations, it's generally better to opt for the latter. For essays, either approach is acceptable.

Tell them how all of the things you've mentioned will result in your conclusion. Here, you should say something to the tune of "points A, B, and C, combined with the response to counterargument X, will result in conclusion Z."

If you want, you can end your introduction with a sentence to lead into your first point. However, this isn't always necessary since you can introduce your first point at the start of the next paragraph.

On top of this, make sure that you don't discuss any ideas that won't be referred to throughout your argument. These kinds of red herrings can set false expectations for the reader or audience, and can ultimately make your argument more confusing. This is why we suggest writing your introduction after you've finished writing the main body of work – once you have all of it written, you'll know which ideas to include in your introduction.

The length of your introduction will vary depending on how long your body of work is. For shorter essays and arguments, your introduction shouldn't be any longer than the paragraphs in the main body of your argument. Additionally, your introduction should only be a paragraph long. As a general rule, if your introduction is so long that it needs to be split into more than one paragraph, then it's probably *too* long. There may of course be a few exceptions where it is appropriate to divide your introduction into two paragraphs, but these are the exception rather than the rule.

When delivering a verbal argument in a debating scenario the same rules apply. The likelihood is that you will prepare the introduction to your argument beforehand, with at least a few bullet points that you can read and string together. In other scenarios, such as less formal arguments, an introduction won't be necessary. Use your intuition in these cases to figure out whether you need an introduction, or if you're better off jumping straight into your argument.

Exit Stage Left – Writing the Perfect Conclusion

The only way to round off a great body of work is with a conclusion. Conclusions are vital for the following reasons:

1. They remind your reader or audience of everything you've covered in your argument, so that they can visualise the path that your piece has taken.

2. You can re-contextualise every point that you've made, bringing them all together for the end.

The best conclusions are ones which bring the reader back to the beginning, giving them a moment to recap on everything that they've read, whilst reiterating the driving point of your argument. If you've written your argument well, the reader or audience shouldn't have had a significant issue following everything you've said, but rounding it off in a conclusion is a good idea anyway. Even if the recap isn't entirely necessary because your argument was easy to follow, it gives the argument some closure.

When it comes to writing your conclusion, make use of the same three points we discussed in the previous section on introductions: **clarity, accuracy, and brevity**. While your conclusion serves a very different function to the introduction, they should both be approached in a similar fashion.

- **Clarity** – In clear language, remind the reader of what you've already covered, and how all of this connects to your main point of argument.

- **Accuracy** – Using the terms that you've defined, bring your argument to a close.

- **Brevity** – Don't waffle on for long about irrelevant details. Summarise your argument in as few words as possible.

On top of these three guidelines, here are a few more tips for crafting the perfect conclusion.

Don't Introduce New Ideas

As mentioned before, one of the worst things you can do when writing a conclusion is to bring in a new idea. If your argument contained ideas *A*, *B*, *C*, and *D*, you should only refer to these ideas **only** in your conclusion. If you haven't discussed an idea already in your argument, **do not** introduce it in your conclusion.

If it's really such an important concept that you might have missed, go back and try and find a place for it. Otherwise, leave it out. Introducing new ideas in the conclusion has the effect of making your argument look rushed or poorly considered.

Don't Get Grandiose

Just like how grand-standing can weaken your introduction, grandiose statements in your conclusion waste space and time, whilst offering nothing to your argument. It's fine to have a bit of flair, and perhaps hint at the greater implications of your argument, but don't act as though your argument is the most profound thing in the world. Some humility will go a long way, and make your argument seem more sophisticated, as opposed to melodramatic.

Conclusion

Now you should have a good idea about how to construct great introductions and conclusions to act as bookends for arguments. When writing your introductions and conclusions, keep the following in mind:

- Write your introduction and conclusion *after* the rest of your work. This way, you'll know exactly what to include in both of them.

- Avoid grand-standing in your introductions and conclusions. Stick to the point and get rid of any unnecessary waffle.

- Keep your introductions and conclusions as short as possible whilst also including all of the core, necessary components.

- Don't introduce any new ideas in your conclusion. If it's important enough that it needs mentioning, find a place for it in the main body of your argument.

IMPROVING YOUR MEMORY

One of the best ways to succeed in a 24-hour essay is to have great memory. This means you can spend less time flicking back and forth through research and notes, and have more time to write your argument. In this chapter, we'll be looking at ways in which you can improve your short-term and long-term memory so that writing a killer essay in 24 hours is even more feasible.

Preferably, you want to be able to look at your notes, read the quote or data that you need, and then quickly enter it into your essay. Likewise, having a strong long-term memory will give you an edge when remembering important facts from your lectures. If you can remember all of the little details, you can save time on note-taking and more on developing your own ideas.

Take note that not all of these tips will explicitly help you on your current essay, but will instead give you the tools to complete future essays in a shorter space of time. Essentially, improving your long-term memory so that you can easily remember information, ideas, facts, and viewpoints will make your next essay flow naturally, rather than it feeling like you're just regurgitating notes from a book.

How Does Memory Work?

While neuroscientists haven't uncovered all of the mysteries regarding the brain, the mind, and consciousness, we have a good understanding of how memories are formed and stored in the brain. In this chapter, we'll be taking a look at the physical elements of memory, such as which processes create memories as well as where memories are held. Then, we'll be moving onto helpful ways about thinking of memory and how it works – ways that will hopefully give you a better understanding of where you need to improve in your studying.

Memory – It's all in Your Head

While there are still mysteries about memory, neuroscientists have a good idea about how it works. To start with, long-term memories seem to be stored in the hippocampus, a part of the brain. Memories are formed when neurons in the brain make connections with each other – connections that are never broken. There are millions of neurons in your brain, and each will make many connections to other neurons. This means that you'll be able to retain potentially billions of memories during your lifetime. So, you don't really need to worry about running out of space. As far as we can currently tell, short-term memories don't involve any physical changes in the brain – this only occurs when a long-term memory is created.

The reason why it's important to know about how the brain itself deals with memories is that it allows you to find out what lifestyle changes allow for you to improve your memory. In particular, some studies suggest that different foods and activities can stimulate the hippocampus and potentially even strengthen connections made between neurons. While this might not mean that eating certain foods will guarantee a better memory, it might be worth looking into.

Useful Ways to Think About Memory

While learning about how the brain works is fascinating and useful in some ways, it isn't entirely helpful just to think of your memory as a billion neurons making connections. Thankfully, some psychologists have specialised in creating models of memory that attempt to describe how it feels for us to create and store memories.

While there's some dispute over which model is the most accurate, they can still be helpful ways of thinking about memory so that it's easier to understand.

You might have noticed that, so far, we've referred to 'short-term' and 'long-term' memory. This is a popular way of thinking about memory, but it isn't entirely accepted across the board by psychologists. Some researchers disagree on whether short-term and long-term memory are two distinct systems in the brain, but instead are a single unit. Whatever the case, it appears that the brain can temporarily hold some memory, and also store it for longer periods of time while also being able to manipulate it to some degree.

So, short-term memory seems to be the place where memories are first stored upon creation. Some people refer to this as 'working memory' since it's the information that you're using in the current moment. There isn't a complete consensus on how much the short-term memory can hold and for how long, but studies show that information in your short-term memory tends to last between 15 and 30 seconds. This is fine when you need to remember a phone number for a few seconds, or remember which cupboard your food goes in, but it isn't particularly useful for remembering large portions of information.

For studying, you really want to make use of your long-term memory. Long-term memory is different for a number of reasons. Firstly, the creation of long-term memories involves physical changes in the brain. When a long-term memory is formed, more connections are made between the neurons inside your brain. In addition, long-term memory is held permanently, whilst short-term memories can only be held for a limited amount of time. Even if you can't remember it anymore, it's likely that the memories are still in your brain somewhere – you're just having difficulty recalling them.

It might be helpful to think of your long-term memory as a massive hard drive, filled with all kinds of information. Life events, facts, as well as instructions on how to perform certain actions, are all stored in here. As time progresses, you'll gather more memories, meaning that your brain ends up storing a lot of information. Naturally, some memories will be used less than others, and these ones tend to be harder to recall. Essentially, the more you use a memory, the easier it will be to recall.

This might be why most revision techniques encourage you to repeat phrases, or recall them on the spot (e.g. flashcards). When revising, bear this in mind – make sure you're recalling all the information you've learned, so that it will be easier to do so when you're writing your essay. It also seems that you're more likely to remember something if you're in an environment that you originally learned it in, or had an experience in. For example, if you first experienced driving in a certain city, you'll likely be reminded of it when you revisit that same place. This means that sitting practice papers in a controlled environment might be useful for remembering things.

How can I Improve my Memory?

Your brain can store huge amounts of information, so you don't need to worry about expanding the capacity of your brain. The brain has approximately a billion neurons in it, and each of these can form over one thousand connections to other neurons. This means that there are over a trillion connections in the human brain. If each of these connections accounts for a single memory, then that means your brain can store one trillion memories.

If this is true, you don't need to worry about your brain running out of storage space.

Instead, people who want to improve their memory need to focus on the following:

- Making sure information is committed to long-term memory;

- Finding reliable ways to recall these memories easily.

We'll be taking a look at both of these in more detail, looking at tricks which you can use to improve in both areas.

Sending Information to Long-Term Memory

As we've discussed, information starts by existing in the short-term memory. This is where memories you need in the moment are kept, and can only last reliably for up to 30 seconds. After this, they either disappear entirely or become inaccurate.

For this reason, you need to make sure the information you're absorbing in your revision enters the long-term memory. Lots of things get stored in your long-term memory without much conscious effort on your part, but this doesn't mean you can read a page once and expect it all to be absorbed.

You need to focus on the information and use techniques to create strong connections. A lot of people find that associating information with certain things can be useful. Rewriting information in your own words, or discussing it in your own words with a friend, is usually a good way of committing information to long-term memory. You'll associate facts with where you are and who you're talking to, and rewording the information will prove that you understand it.

There are a few other methods, all with some scientific evidence, which allow you to strengthen memories and commit them more easily. Scientists have found a connection between chewing gum while studying and committing more memories to long-term memory, potentially because chewing gum stimulates the hippocampus (the part of the brain which handles memory). Other studies suggest that drinking coffee helps consolidation of information to long-term memory.

However, remember that a dependence on caffeine can put you at a disadvantage when you're in the exam room. Finally, some studies suggest that eating berries can improve your ability to commit information to the long-term memory. This might be worth trying if you want to gain an extra advantage when it comes to studying.

Improving Recollection

Once you've committed things to long-term memory, you need to work on recollection techniques. As previously mentioned, memories that get used often end up being easier to recall. For example, you can probably remember things like your telephone number, home address, or internet passwords easily because you write, say, or type them a lot. Think about your passwords that are saved automatically. When you eventually have to type them in again, are they more difficult to remember? If this is the case for you, then it's because you haven't had to recall it as much.

So, one of the best ways to improve recollection is to test yourself regularly. Almost every revision tactic does this, but the ones that are best suited for this are flashcards, reciting key facts out loud, learning games, and mind maps. Try and do these without looking at your notes so that you can test how strong your ability to recall is.

There are a few other methods which also help to improve recall, including some lifestyle changes. Some studies show that both meditation and exercise can help to strengthen your recall ability. In addition, getting a good night's sleep regularly has been linked to stronger memory. Try these for yourself and see how they work for you.

On top of memories being easier to recall if they're used often, some studies show that creating strong associations between things can make memories easier to recall. For a moment, think of your brain as an attic or large storage locker, and all of the objects inside it represent memories. The ones closest to the entrance are the ones you take out and put back in most regularly, so they're the easiest to recall. However, what about the belongings at the back? Getting to those, or even being able to see them in the darkness, can prove to be incredibly difficult. Now imagine tying a piece of rope to each of these objects, and leaving the loose end near the entrance of the locker. You could follow each of these to find the objects at the back of the room. These pieces of rope represent associations made in your mind, so that these memories are easier to recall.

Tips for Improving Your Memory

A good place to start when working to improve your memory is your everyday routine. By this, we mean that adjusting your lifestyle choices in several little ways can improve memory retention and recollection.

While the following tips seem simple, it cannot be understated just how important they are if you want to see fast improvement in your mental sharpness!

1. Cementing sleep

Of course, getting enough sleep is an essential part of maintaining both your physical and mental health. Therefore, nailing down a good 8 hours goes hand-in-hand with having a good memory! Not only this, though, but memories become cemented in our minds during an undisturbed sleep, making REM sleep incredibly important for the retention of the day's events in the brain.

2. Exercise those cells

One of the most important reasons to exercise is for the boost in brain function. Physical exertion helps to maintain the health of brain cells, and even serves to stimulate the development of new blood vessels in the brain. This all serves to increase how much information you can store in your brain, as well as how quickly you can recall it.

3. Water work

Drinking enough water is a very easy act of self-care to neglect, but one that has a widespread impact should you do so. Dehydration is disastrous for cognitive function – studies have shown that even being slightly dehydrated can restrict how much information we are able to take in and process. The NHS recommends that to be at peak performance, you should drink around 1.5 to 2 litres of water per day. Of course, alcohol consumption is tied to memory loss, and for good reason. Cutting down can reduce nitrates, which are tied to unhappy brains!

4. Brain food

Similarly, there are certain foods that you should look at if you want to improve your memory, as well as some that you should avoid! You won't be too surprised by what you see here! Leafy vegetables and fruit are ones that are known to aid cognitive function, while wholegrains are believed to aid concentration, which in turn will help how well you can retain and recall information. Foods like white bread and processed meat bring toxins into the body, which can impair efficient brain function.

5. Destress yourself

Taking steps to reduce your general stress levels will benefit you on your quest to improve your memory, for one simple reason. When you are feeling stressed, it is because your brain has triggered the production of 'stress hormones'. While this is happening, some other brain functions are suppressed, including the formation of lucid memories. In other words, when you're stressed, your brain does not prioritise solidifying your experiences of the day as memories in your head! So, don't be so hard on yourself, take time to unwind every day.

Now the basics are out of the way, let's go onto the specific techniques you can employ when aiming to memorise any amount of content you need to know.

Create representations in your brain

This method of making associations is most common, and can be applied to almost any kind of information with a bit of ingenuity. Essentially, you want to give your own meaning to facts and data by representing them in a unique way. For example, if you needed to remember that the Easter Rising in Ireland occurred in 1916, you could imagine a pile of Easter eggs going up in an elevator to floor 1916. This might seem bizarre, but these types of association can help you remember important details more easily. If you're any good at drawing, it might even help to make brief sketches for the most important things you need to know!

Chunking

Chunking is the process of chopping up larger pieces of information into smaller pieces, so that you can remember them more easily. This is particularly useful for things like phone numbers, but can also be used for academic study too. For example, say that you need to memorise a mathematical formula or method for solving a certain kind of maths problem. You could dissect the whole solution into smaller steps, then memorise the process. Then, you can apply the above method for creating representations for each step, or use the method of loci (explained below).

Method of Loci

This is a technique that dates all the way back to the ancient Greeks and Romans, and involves mentally visualising locations and attaching information to them.

First, think of a familiar place, such as your bedroom, classroom, or office. Alternatively, you can imagine a route that you take regularly, like your commute to work or school. Then, start to imagine placing the information you need to remember in this environment, such as key dates or names. Once you've done this, try to keep the location in your mind. This means that, when you think of this location, you'll also be able to recall the memories that you've 'placed' there.

Conclusion

In this chapter, we've taken a look at how memory works, as well as ways to improve your memory. In particular, candidates who want to make sure that their memory is at its peak should focus on improving their recollection, since this will greatly improve your ability to work quickly without having to constantly refer to your notes while writing the essay.

CONCLUSION

You've now reached the end of *Rapid Skills for Students: 24 Hours to a First Class Essay.* By using this book, you've given yourself the skills necessary to research, plan, and write an essay which is sophisticated and robust – a huge bonus for students looking to up their game academically – all in the space of 24 hours. Bear the information in this book in mind whilst planning your work.

A Few Final Words...

For any challenge, it is helpful to keep the following in mind...

The Three 'P's

1. Preparation. Preparation is key to passing any test or essay; you won't be doing yourself any favours by not taking the time to prepare. Many fail at university because they did not know what to expect or did not know what their own weaknesses were. Take the time to go over any areas you may have struggled with. By doing this, you will become familiar with how you will perform when it comes to writing your essay.

2. Perseverance. If you set your sights on a goal and stick to it, you are more likely to succeed. Obstacles and setbacks are common when trying to achieve something great, and you shouldn't shy away from them. Instead, face the tougher parts of your course even if you feel defeated. If you need to, take a break from your work to relax and then return with renewed vigour. If you fail the test or essay, take the time to consider why you failed, gather your strength and try again.

3. Performance. How well you perform will be the result of your preparation and perseverance. Remember to relax when taking the test and try not to panic. Believe in your own abilities, practise as much as you can, and motivate yourself constantly. Nothing is gained without hard work and determination, and this applies to your university course as much as anything else in life.

We wish you the best of luck in all of your future endeavours!

Get Access To

FREE Psychometric

Tests

www.PsychometricTestsOnline.co.uk

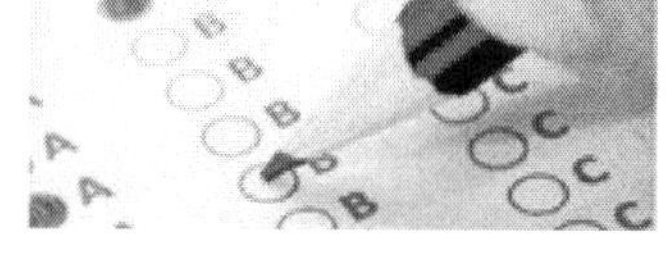

Printed and bound by CPI Group (UK) Ltd, Croydon, CR0 4YY

06/07/2026

02157570-0004